Think And Have Pee

Life Lessons, Mental Detox, and Deep
Thoughts from the Bathroom of Wisdom

Table of Contents

INTRODUCTION 4

CHAPTER 1 EVERYONE THINKS... AND EVERYONE PEES 7

CHAPTER 2 THE FULL TANK PROBLEM 10

CHAPTER 3 HOW THE MIND BECOMES OVERCROWDED 13

CHAPTER 4 OVERTHINKING: THE SILENT PEE-HOLDING CHAMPION 19

CHAPTER 5 EMOTIONAL CONSTIPATION: HOLDING IN WHAT SHOULD BE LET GO 26

CHAPTER 6 THE MIND'S BATHROOM: WHERE THOUGHTS GO TO WAIT 33

CHAPTER 7 LETTING GO BEFORE YOU BURST 41

CHAPTER 8 THE FREEDOM OF EMPTYING THE MIND 49

CHAPTER 9 FLUSH THE PAST: CLEARING WHAT NO LONGER SERVES YOU 57

CHAPTER 10 THE BATHROOM OF ENLIGHTENMENT 65

CHAPTER 11 PHILOSOPHERS, SUFIS & ZEN MASTERS: MASTERS OF THE MENTAL PEE   73

CHAPTER 12 PRESSURE IS NOT THE ENEMY AVOIDANCE IS   82

CHAPTER 13 THINK LIGHT, LIVE LIGHT   90

CHAPTER 14 THE JOY OF RELIEF: WHY RELEASE FEELS SO GOOD   99

CHAPTER 15 THE FLOW PHILOSOPHY: LET WHAT COMES COME, LET WHAT GOES GO   108

CHAPTER 16 THINK AND HAVE PEE (THE FINAL REALIZATION)   117

EPILOGUE WHEN THE MIND FINALLY BREATHES   126

AUTHOR'S NOTE   128

DEDICATION PAGE   129

FURTHER READING BY SHAMAIL AIJAZ   130

INTRODUCTION

Why This Book Exists: Because Your Mind Is Full and So Are You

Human beings carry an invisible weight that grows heavier the longer we pretend it isn't there. On the surface, we appear civilized smartphones in hand, responsibilities stacked like towers, deadlines orbiting us like impatient satellites. Yet beneath all that sophistication exists a simple, ancient truth: **we are creatures of pressure.** Thoughts, worries, memories, expectations, guilt, overanalysis, unfinished conversations, doubts, dreams all of them collect inside the mind the same way water fills a tank. At first, the weight is manageable. Then it becomes uncomfortable. Then it becomes unbearable. And when you finally release it, the sense of relief is so profound that you wonder why you held it in for so long.

That relief the heavenly exhale that makes the world lighter is not limited to biology. It is a mental phenomenon too. The mind is a bathroom with no schedule and endless visitors. Thoughts enter without knocking, sit wherever they want, and refuse to leave. Some latch onto guilt and rehearse old punishments. Others cling to fear and whisper worst-case scenarios. Some replay the same memory until it becomes a form of self-imposed torture. A few keep showing up simply because they're bored. And all this time, you are left trying to hold your balance while the pressure inside keeps rising.

This book was born from observing this human condition with humor instead of despair. Because when you look at the mind honestly, you'll notice something oddly funny: **we take our thoughts far more seriously than they deserve.** One moment the mind convinces you that the world is ending because you misplaced your charger. The next moment it declares you a failure because someone didn't reply to your message. The mind does not negotiate; it narrates. And when that narration goes unchecked, the internal pressure becomes overwhelming. Yet, ironically, the mind that creates the pressure also holds the key to releasing it.

What if mental clarity wasn't about controlling your thoughts, but learning how to *let them flow*? What if thinking wasn't a burden but a privilege something that becomes lighter the moment you stop trying to force every idea into order? And what if the greatest wisdom in life was understanding the simple art of "release" before the tank overflows? These questions form the foundation of **Think and Have Pee** a humorous yet philosophical exploration into how the mind works, why it fills up, and how to empty it without losing the essence of who you are.

Life becomes harder when you hold in things meant to be released anger, fear, resentment, unnecessary thoughts, someone else's expectations, or yesterday's arguments. Most people spend their whole lives clenching their inner world tightly, believing that control equals strength. But real strength is the ability to let go at the right moment. It is the courage to unclench the fist the mind keeps closing. It is the wisdom to realize that a full mind is not a sign of knowledge; it is a sign of congestion.

You are not meant to carry everything. You are meant to understand what to keep, what to flush, and what to let flow like a river that never apologizes for moving forward. This book won't preach spirituality with a straight face; it will make you laugh while guiding you toward clarity. Because humor opens the door that seriousness keeps locked. When you laugh, you relax. And when you relax, the truth finally has enough space to walk in.

By the time you finish this journey, the philosophy will feel simple: **Think freely, feel lightly, release often, and let nothing stay inside longer than it should.** Your mind will always generate new thoughts. That is its nature. But your peace depends on learning when to let them go. As you read these chapters, carry this idea gently: the mind is not a container to be filled endlessly, it is a river, a stream, a flow. And everything that flows must be allowed to move.

"The mind becomes peaceful the moment you stop holding what was never meant to stay."

CHAPTER 1 Everyone Thinks... and Everyone Pees

Because No Matter How Royal, Rich, Wise, or Wild You Are... Biology and Thoughts Treat Everyone the Same

There are two things every human on this planet does, no matter how extraordinary they believe themselves to be: **they think**, and **they pee**. Strip away the layers of titles, wealth, ego, medals, and job descriptions, and what remains is a creature wired to produce thoughts and pressure with the same reliability as sunrise. Nobody is spared. Kings do it, monks do it, astronauts do it, CEOs do it, philosophers do it, even the neighbor who thinks he is spiritually superior because he once read a book on mindfulness does it. Every single human without exception faces the daily cycle of mental buildup and physical release.

This simple biological truth creates the first philosophical insight of this book: **we are far less different than we imagine.**
No matter how impressive someone appears on the outside, their internal life is a mess of thoughts, doubts, urges, and impulses just like yours. Their mind wanders, panics, overthinks, creates imaginary problems, runs simulations of conversations that will never happen, and argues with people who don't even know they are part of the argument. We pretend everyone else has their life together while we alone suffer from chaos inside. But look

closely, and you'll see that humanity is a giant community of people trying to hold themselves together while their minds produce nonsense at the speed of light.

And this is where pee comes in not as a joke, but as a metaphor for equality and humility. When you forget that someone else is human, just remember they also feel pressure, they also seek relief, and they also experience the desperate urgency of **"I need to sort myself out right now."** Thoughts do the same thing. They show up uninvited, pile up without permission, and demand your attention at the most inconvenient moments. Thoughts are like biological pressure: they don't care if you're busy, if you're in a meeting, or if you're pretending to be a calm, evolved version of yourself.

In fact, one reason people struggle with their inner world is that they expect the mind to behave. But the mind is not here to behave; it is here to create movement. Trying to stop your thoughts is like trying to stop your bladder from ever filling again you're fighting a natural process. The more you resist, the more pressure you create. The more pressure you create, the more miserable you become. And the more miserable you become, the more you begin to believe that something is wrong with you, when the truth is far more comforting: **you're just human.**

Thoughts don't come to remind you that you're broken; they come to remind you that you're alive. They are the background hum of existence, the constant stream of awareness, imagination, memory, and curiosity. But you were never meant to store every thought. You were meant to let them pass through you the same way your body lets go of what it no longer needs. Every thought is temporary unless you decide to hold it, replay it, cling to it, or obsess over it. Then it becomes a burden, not by nature, but by choice.

The beauty of understanding this simple truth is freedom. When you stop treating your thoughts as emergencies, you begin to see them as passing clouds in a sky that was yours long before they arrived. The mind becomes lighter, the emotional load becomes softer, and life stops feeling like a private battle you must win. Instead, you see yourself as part of a universal human comedy billions of people pretending to have it all together while secretly navigating the same cycle of pressure and release.

Humility begins when illusion ends. And the greatest illusion is the belief that others are stable while you are chaotic. No, everyone is chaotic. Everyone is overwhelmed. Everyone is trying. And everyone, at some point today, will be relieved physically or mentally after holding something longer than they should have.

By accepting this truth, you remove the shame of being human. You allow yourself to laugh at the absurdity of existence and finally relax into the shared experience of being alive. This shared truth is where connection begins, compassion grows, and clarity finally finds space to enter.

"The first step toward wisdom is accepting that everyone is human even the people who pretend they aren't."

CHAPTER 2   The Full Tank Problem

Why the Mind Fills Faster Than Life Can Empty It

There is a precise moment in every human day when the mind feels heavier than the body when the pressure inside begins to rise, not because of what is happening around you, but because of what is happening within you. The thoughts you didn't address yesterday return today wearing heavier clothes. The anxieties you ignored politely knock again, this time louder. The unspoken words, postponed decisions, and lingering doubts all form a silent queue inside your mind, waiting for acknowledgment, resolution, or release. This inner buildup, invisible yet powerful, is what we call **The Full Tank Problem.**

Just like the body creates pressure when the bladder fills, the mind creates pressure when thoughts accumulate. The difference is this: the body sends clear signals tightness, discomfort, urgency while the mind sends subtle ones. Restlessness. Irritation. Confusion. Snapping at small things. Feeling overwhelmed by tasks that were easy yesterday. Overreacting to a single comment. Losing patience with yourself or the world for no obvious reason. These are not personality flaws; these are pressure warnings. Your mind is full. Your tank is rising. Your internal system is politely saying, "Excuse me... something needs to be released."

But most people ignore these early signals. They try to "hold it in" mentally the same way they hold in physical pressure, believing that endurance is strength. They imagine that pushing through will make everything disappear. Instead, the tank keeps filling until the weight becomes unbearable. And when it finally overflows, the reaction surprises even the person experiencing it: the sudden outburst, the unexpected breakdown, the emotional explosion that seems too big for the situation. This is not sudden. It is accumulated. It is everything you didn't release, asking to be released all at once.

A full mind behaves like a full tank:

- **Every small thing feels bigger.**
- **Every delay feels personal.**
- **Every mistake feels catastrophic.**
- **Every conversation feels heavier than it should.**

Because when your tank is full, *everything* becomes pressure.

The trouble is that society rewards "holding it together." We praise the calm face, the controlled demeanor, the person who says "I'm fine" even when their internal world is on fire. We admire the quiet sufferer more than the honest releaser. But there is nothing noble about overflowing silently. The mind was designed to process thoughts, not store them forever. When you treat thinking as a burden instead of a flow, pressure becomes your lifestyle.

Imagine a smartphone with a hundred apps running in the background. The phone becomes slow, hot, and irresponsive yet nothing is technically wrong with it. It just needs a reset, not a repair. The human mind is the same. Most of your exhaustion doesn't come from what you are doing, but from what you are holding. The mental apps that never close old memories, unprocessed emotions, imaginary fears, unnecessary worries. They run quietly, draining your clarity byte by byte.

The Full Tank Problem becomes dangerous only when you forget that you have the power to release pressure. The moment you acknowledge the buildup; the mind begins to soften. But denial tightens the grip. People often say, "I don't have time to deal with this right now." What they mean is, "I don't know how to release this without falling apart." But falling apart is not the only option. Letting go is a controlled release. It is not weakness; it is maintenance.

You were never meant to carry every thought. You were meant to choose which ones deserve space. A full tank does not make you wise it makes you heavy. A flowing mind, however, makes you alive. The art is not in preventing the tank from filling. It is in learning how to release long before it overflows.

"Life doesn't drown you with pressure; it only reminds you to release what you were never meant to hold."

CHAPTER 3 How the Mind Becomes Overcrowded

The Silent Conspiracy Between Memory, Emotion, and Imagination

There is a strange phenomenon that every human mind experiences but rarely understands: the gradual overcrowding of thoughts, emotions, fears, fantasies, and unprocessed moments. At first, the mind seems spacious like a clean room with a window open. Thoughts enter, explore for a moment, then leave politely. But as life becomes heavier, the mind begins to behave like a train station during peak hours. Thoughts rush in faster than they leave, bumping into each other, dropping emotional luggage everywhere, arguing for attention, and creating a noise that feels impossible to quiet down. The question is: **How does this happen? How does a mind that starts peacefully becoming a marketplace of chaos?**

To understand overcrowding, you must first understand the three biggest culprits' memory, emotion, and imagination. These three, when separate, serve a purpose. But when they form alliances, they behave like uninvited guests who overstay their welcome, rearrange the furniture, and then ask why you're stressed.

1. Memory: The Hoarder of the Mind

Memory was designed as a tool to help you avoid danger, learn from patterns, and recognize beauty. But somewhere along the evolutionary timeline, memory started collecting everything not just meaningful moments, but every embarrassment, disappointment, rejection, and awkward handshake you've had since childhood. It stores even the smallest fragments of past discomfort and waits for the perfect moment to replay them: preferably 2 a.m., preferably when you're tired, preferably when you can't do anything about it.

Memory never asks, *"Does this still matter?"* It simply says, *"It happened once, so let's keep it forever."*

This is how the overcrowding begins.
Not from new thoughts, but from old ones refusing to leave.

Most people don't realize that the brain is less like a library and more like a refrigerator. It was meant to store fresh items for short periods and do not keep every leftover emotion until it starts to smell. But because humans don't know how to "throw away" emotional leftovers, the mind becomes filled with stale thoughts disguised as important ones.

2. Emotion: The Amplifier

Emotion doesn't create clutter; it inflates it. A neutral memory becomes heavy when emotion gives it weight. An uncertain future becomes terrifying when emotion adds imagination. Emotion builds attachments to thoughts that never deserved to stay. It convinces you that something is urgent when it isn't, dangerous when it's ordinary, and permanent when it's temporary.

Emotion takes a thought and shouts into a microphone:
"THIS IS IMPORTANT!"
And because the voice comes from within you, you believe it.

This internal megaphone is why certain worries, fears, or memories feel bigger than life. Emotion doesn't care about logic. It cares about intensity. And intensity fills space.

3. Imagination: The Hyperactive Roommate

If memory is the hoarder and emotion is the amplifier, imagination is the over-energetic roommate who never sleeps. It runs ahead of reality, painting dramatic movies of things that haven't happened and probably never will.

- One small mistake becomes a disaster.
- One uncertain future becomes a catastrophe.
- One unanswered message becomes a rejection.
- One unfamiliar sound becomes danger.

Imagination creates "ghost thoughts" ideas that have no basis in reality but feel real because emotion fuels them.

This is mental overcrowding at its finest:
Memory stores old stuff,
Emotion intensifies it,
Imagination adds new fears on top.

Before you know it, your mind becomes a crowded room where everybody believes it is the main character.

Why Thoughts Don't Leave on Their Own

In the physical world, guests eventually get tired and go home. In the mind, thoughts do not leave unless you *release* them deliberately. They stay because you feed them attention. Even a single moment of worry can give a thought enough energy to stick around for years.

Thoughts follow a simple rule:
What you ignore stays. What you observe moves.

Overcrowding happens because people try to suppress their thoughts instead of acknowledging them. Suppression is like trapping emotions in a storage room. Acknowledgment is like opening the door and letting them walk out.

But modern life encourages suppression.
"Stay busy."
"Don't think about it."
"Move on."
"Be strong."

All noble phrases, but all terrible strategies.

The mind is not a dam; it is a river. It does not need walls, it needs flow.

Why the Mind Creates More Than It Can Handle

People assume overcrowding happens because too many things happen in life. But the truth is more ironic: **the mind generates far more thoughts than reality requires.**

Reality gives you one event.
The mind creates thirty interpretations of that event.
Emotion intensifies ten of those interpretations.
Imagination exaggerates five of them into full-blown panic.
Memory stores all of them.

This is how a single moment becomes a lifelong tenant.

Your mind was never designed for this much content. It evolved in a world where thoughts were simple food, safety, tribe, survival. Today, the mind is attacked by notifications, expectations, deadlines, comparisons, and unending sensory input.

It's not overcrowding by choice; it's overcrowding by design.

The Comedy in All This Chaos

Look at your mind with humor for a moment. It collects old arguments. It holds imaginary conversations. It worries about events that never happened. It rehearses responses you will never say. It creates future disasters from tiny inconveniences. It remembers embarrassing moments from ten years ago yet can't remember where you put your keys.

Your mind is not broken. It's just dramatic.

It's trying to help, but it overhelps. It tries to protect you by creating unnecessary scenarios. It tries to prepare you by imagining problems that don't exist. It tries to support you by replaying the past. The mind is like a loyal but misguided friend who loves you too much to relax.

Overcrowding isn't failure; its affection gone wrong.

The First Step: Seeing the Crowd

The moment you observe the internal crowd without judgment, space appears. Awareness creates room. When you see the mind's chaos with clarity not resistance you stop feeding it. And when you stop feeding it, it stops growing.

Overcrowding ends when you stop believing that every thought deserves a seat in your life.

Thoughts are passengers, not residents.

Your mind becomes lighter the moment you stop treating every mental visitor like a VIP.

"Your mind becomes overcrowded not because life is heavy, but because you give permanent space to thoughts meant to pass through."

CHAPTER 4 Overthinking: The Silent Pee-Holding Champion

Why the Mind Refuses to Relax Even When the Body Begs for Peace

If the human mind had an Olympics, **overthinking** would win gold every single time. It is the undefeated champion, the one athlete who trains 24 hours a day without rest, running mental marathons nobody asked for, solving problems that never existed, and preparing for disasters that reality itself is too tired to create. Overthinking is not simply thinking too much it is the psychological equivalent of holding your pee long after your body has politely said, "We need to fix this situation immediately."

Most people don't realize how similar the two experiences are. When you hold physical pressure, the body tightens, becomes uncomfortable, impatient, distracted, and oddly dramatic. When you hold on to mental pressure, the same thing happens. The mind becomes restless, rigid, and hyperalert. You begin rehearsing future conversations, making backup plans for imaginary scenarios, and thinking in circles so tight that even your thoughts get dizzy. Holding pee is uncomfortable for the body; holding thoughts is torture for the soul.

Why Overthinking Feels Like Control but Is Actually Panic

The most fascinating thing about overthinking is that people mistake it for intelligence. They believe that the more they think, the more prepared they'll be, the better their decisions will become, and the safer their future will feel. Overthinking disguises itself as responsibility, maturity, and "being careful." But look deeper, and you'll see that overthinking is simply **fear wearing a suit.**

It is not control it is *the illusion* of control.

The brain starts overthinking when it cannot tolerate uncertainty. Instead of facing the unknown with calm curiosity, it tries to outsmart the future by imagining every possible outcome. This does not make you prepared. It makes you exhausted. Overthinking is the mind's way of saying:

"I don't trust myself to handle tomorrow, so let me panic about it today."

And, just like holding pee, the longer you hold your worries, the more uncomfortable everything becomes. You sit, but you cannot rest. You sleep, but your thoughts stay awake. You try to enjoy life, but your mind insists on running an analysis of what could go wrong at breakfast, lunch, and dinner.

Overthinking Turns Molehills into Mountains

An overthinking mind doesn't process information it multiplies it. It takes one small worry and turns it into a trilogy. It takes a simple decision and turns it into an existential crisis. It takes a single doubt and repeats it until your confidence evaporates. Overthinking doesn't make life difficult; it makes **simple things heavy.**

- Someone doesn't reply → They must hate you.
- You make a small mistake → Your whole future is ruined.
- You feel tired → Something is wrong with your life direction.
- Someone speaks softly → They're hiding something.

Even silence becomes suspicious when you're an overthinker.

In reality, most situations are simple. But the mind, especially one addicted to analysis cannot tolerate simplicity. It feels unsafe without something to chew on, something to break apart, something to worry about. Overthinking is hunger without appetite, movement without progress, thinking without direction.

Overthinkers Are Secret Endurance Athletes

Not physically, but mentally. They develop unbelievable stamina for mental pain. While others let go of small worries, overthinkers hold them like fragile glass studying every angle, analyzing every crack, worrying about every outcome. They replay moments. They rewrite conversations. They imagine future disasters. They examine their own thoughts as if they were breakable objects.

This endurance is not strength.
It is survival mode.
It is the mental equivalent of refusing to go to the bathroom for three hours during a long meeting and then pretending everything is perfectly normal.

Overthinkers become so used to discomfort that they forget what a calm mind feels like. Peace becomes foreign. Silence feels suspicious. Relaxation feels unsafe. The mind has forgotten that its natural state is flow, not tension.

The Moment When Overthinking Takes Control

There is always a small moment, often unnoticed when thinking crosses the line into overthinking. It is the moment you stop solving the problem and start cycling through the possibilities. It is the moment you shift from analyzing to imagining. It is the moment when the mind stops being helpful and starts being dramatic.

- Normal thinking asks: "What is happening?"
- Overthinking asks: "What if everything goes wrong?"

The first brings clarity.
The second brings chaos.

Overthinking is triggered not by events, but by interpretations. It is not the problem itself that floods your mind; it is the meaning your mind assigns to the problem.

One rejection becomes "I am not good enough."
One delay becomes "My life is falling apart."
One argument becomes "Everything is ruined."
One uncertainty becomes "I must prepare for the worst."

Overthinking takes reality and paints it with the darkest color in the box.

The Body Knows Before the Mind Does

Here is the interesting part:
Your body always knows when your mind is overthinking.

You may not notice the mental loops, but your body notices the tension. Your shoulders lift. Your jaw tightens. Your breathing becomes shallow. Your stomach clenches. Your heartbeat shifts. These are not random. These are signals physical warnings that the mind is carrying too much.

But instead of releasing pressure, people try to think their way out of their thoughts. This is like trying to empty a full bladder by drinking more water.

The solution is never "think harder."
The solution is always "release what you don't need."

Why Overthinking Never Leads to Enlightenment

People secretly believe that if they overthink long enough, they will arrive at a magical moment of clarity. They imagine the mind offering a perfect answer after hours of analysis. But overthinking does not create clarity; it blocks it. Clarity comes from emptiness, not excess.

Wisdom is found in space, not noise.

The mind must be allowed to breathe. Thought must be allowed to come and go. Insight arises not from the storm of thinking, but from the quiet that follows it.

Overthinking is simply pressure begging to be released. It is the mind saying,

"Please stop holding everything. Let me be."

Overthinking Is Not Your Enemy Your Attachment to It Is

The real problem is not that you overthink; the real problem is that you believe your thoughts are facts. Overthinking becomes dangerous only when you treat every thought like the truth. Most thoughts are temporary visitors. Overthinkers treat them like permanent residents.

In reality, you do not need fewer thoughts.
You need fewer attachments to thoughts.

The mind is naturally active. But suffering begins when you believe that every story it tells must be trusted.

When you detach, thoughts lose power.
When you observe, they lose weight.
When you release, they lose their place in your life.

And just like that
the champion of mental pressure becomes nothing more
than a harmless noise in the distance.

---

*"Overthinking is the mind's attempt to hold
what should have already been released."*

CHAPTER 5 Emotional Constipation: Holding In What Should Be Let Go

Why We Carry Feelings Long After They Expire and How They Quietly Shape Our Lives

There is a peculiar human habit that every culture, every generation, and every individual carries without needing any training: **holding in emotions longer than the mind can handle**. Just as the body becomes uncomfortable when you refuse to release physical pressure, the psyche becomes distressed when you suppress emotional pressure. This discomfort is subtle at first a tightening in the chest, a heaviness behind the ribs, a strange stiffness in your breath. But over time, it becomes something far more disruptive: a persistent internal congestion that clouds judgment, distorts perception, and steals away the natural joy of simply existing. This is what we call **emotional constipation**.

We are taught from childhood how to walk, talk, eat, and read. But nobody teaches us how to release emotions safely. Instead, people receive accidental lessons: "Don't cry," "Be strong," "Move on," "Forget it," "It's not a big deal." These messages, repeated over years, train the mind to store emotions rather than process them. And the result? A generation of people walking around with emotional traffic jams inside them pain stuck behind pride, sadness blocked by denial, fear squeezed between responsibilities, and anger hiding behind forced politeness.

The Strange Burden of Unexpressed Feelings

Unreleased emotions do not disappear; they migrate. They move through the body, occupying whatever space they can find. Some settle in the jaw as tension. Some lodge in the stomach as anxiety. Some sit on the heart like a weight no logic can dissolve. Some hide behind smiles that feel increasingly expensive. You may not be aware of the migration, but your body knows. It keeps score.

Emotional constipation is not about the intensity of feelings but the resistance to them. A small hurt, if resisted, can grow into a giant. A simple disappointment, if suppressed, can evolve into bitterness. A minor conflict, if ignored, can turn into emotional scar tissue. Feelings are like streams they move naturally if you allow them, but they stagnate the moment you try to block their flow.

And stagnation is where suffering begins.

Why Humans Store Emotions Like Expired Groceries

People do not store emotions because they enjoy suffering. They store emotions because **they fear the release more than the pressure.** Society praises emotional restraint so much that expressing feelings begins to look like weakness, immaturity, or loss of control. As a result:

- People swallow their anger to avoid conflict.
- They suppress sadness to appear strong.
- They hide loneliness to avoid appearing needy.
- They mask insecurity with overconfidence.
- They bury guilt under distraction.
- They silence fear with forced logic.

But every emotion suppressed becomes an emotional bill that eventually demands payment. And the cost is always clarity, peace, and authenticity.

The Emotional Toilet Nobody Uses

If the mind had a bathroom for feelings, everyone would be healthier. But society built this bathroom and then locked the door because it feared the mess. Yet the truth remains: **all emotions are temporary if you allow them to pass through.** They only become permanent when you refuse to let them leave.

We don't have emotional constipation because emotions are heavy; we have emotional constipation because we don't know how to let them go.

Imagine if people were taught emotional hygiene the same way they are taught physical hygiene: identifying emotional discomfort early, acknowledging it, and releasing it before it becomes painful. The world would be filled with balanced, calm, emotionally literate individuals. Instead, most people grow up pretending they don't feel what they actually feel. And the more they pretend, the heavier the mind becomes.

The Silent Symptoms of Emotional Constipation

You can detect emotional constipation not by dramatic outbursts but by subtle patterns that build slowly:

- You feel irritated by things that never bothered you before.
- Small tasks suddenly feel overwhelming.
- You become hyper-aware of mistakes.
- People's opinions begin to affect you more.
- You avoid quiet moments because they amplify inner noise.
- You overthink simple decisions.
- Your body feels tense even when life is calm.

These are not flaws; they are signals. The emotional pressure is rising. Something inside wants to leave but doesn't know how.

The danger is not the feeling itself it is the fear of feeling it.

When You Hold Feelings, They Start Holding You

A strange phenomenon occurs the longer you hold a feeling: it begins to shape your identity. You start believing you *are* the sadness you refused to express. You begin thinking you *are* the anger you never released. You assume you *are* the fear you avoided for years.

Unexpressed emotion becomes woven into your personality, not because it belongs there, but because it had nowhere else to go.

You do not become who you truly are you become who your suppressed emotions force you to be.

This is why emotional constipation can change the course of a life. It alters relationships, self-worth, choices, dreams, reactions, and habits. Emotional suppression doesn't just hide feelings; it reshapes the entire inner landscape.

The Philosophy of Emotional Release

To release emotion, you must understand something fundamental: **emotions are messengers, not enemies.** They come with news:

- Sadness says, *"Something mattered."*
- Anger says, *"A boundary was crossed."*
- Fear says, *"I want to feel safe."*
- Guilt says, *"I violated my own values."*
- Love says, *"I recognize something meaningful."*

Every emotion carries wisdom. But when you suppress them, you reject the message and keep only the weight.

Releasing emotions is not dramatic. It is silent, gentle, humane. It begins with acknowledgment, continues with acceptance, and ends with letting go without clinging to the story around it. The moment you stop fighting a feeling, it softens. The moment you allow yourself to feel it fully, it begins to dissolve. Every emotion wants one thing: **to pass.**

It is the resistance that traps it.

Emotional Release Is Not Weakness It Is Maintenance

The strongest minds are not the ones that feel the least; they are the ones that allow feelings to move freely. A mind that represses emotion becomes rigid and fragile. A mind that processes emotion becomes flexible and wise.

Just as muscles grow through tension and release, the psyche grows through feeling and letting go.

We train the body.
We train the intellect.
We train our careers.
But almost nobody trains emotional flow.

Yet emotional literacy is the foundation of mental freedom. Without it, all thoughts become heavier than necessary.

Humor: The Hidden Doorway to Emotional Release

One of the most surprising tools for releasing emotion is humor. Laughter shakes the body, loosens emotional knots, softens the mind, and releases pressure silently. It is emotional stretching disguised as entertainment. A single moment of genuine laughter can do more emotional cleansing than hours of overanalysis.

Humor helps us take the human condition lightly. It allows us to look at our suffering with compassionate distance. It reminds us that we are not broken we are simply alive.

Humor is relief.
Relief is healing.
Healing is release.

The Beginning of Ease

Emotional constipation ends the moment you stop pretending you don't feel what you feel. When you become honest with yourself, the inner traffic begins to move. The congestion loosens. The mind breathes. The heart softens. And life suddenly feels lighter without anything outside you changing.

Release is not an event.
It is a practice.
It is the art of not carrying what isn't meant to be carried.

> *"The emotions you resist don't weaken they wait. And the moment you allow them to pass, they show you the freedom that was always yours."*

CHAPTER 6 The Mind's Bathroom: Where Thoughts Go to Wait

A Humorous Journey Into the Inner Waiting Room Where Every Worry, Memory, and Idea Stands in Line

Inside every human mind exists a secret room a place you never see but constantly feel. It is crowded, noisy, dramatic, unpredictable, and sometimes absurd. This room is where thoughts gather the moment they form, even before you consciously notice them. Some come casually. Others arrive in emergencies. A few walk in with arrogance as if they own the place. Many more arrive uninvited. This is the **Mind's Bathroom**, the silent internal waiting room where thoughts stand in line, tapping their metaphorical feet, waiting for you to acknowledge them, process them, or release them.

This chapter is about entering that room not to clean it, not to control it, but to observe its strange, beautiful, chaotic truth. To understand the mind, you must understand how thoughts behave once they arrive. And trust me, they behave like impatient customers waiting for service: dramatic, demanding, and often ridiculous.

The Mind's Bathroom Is Always Open

Unlike a real bathroom, which mercifully has doors, schedules, locks, and rules, the mind's bathroom is open 24/7. Thoughts walk in whenever they want:

- While you're working
- While you're eating
- While you're trying to sleep
- While you're trying not to think
- While you're waiting for someone to reply
- While you're doing absolutely nothing

They do not knock. They do not ask for permission. They simply show up.

Some thoughts enter gently, like a guest making polite conversation. Others burst in like someone late for an exam. A few come dragging old memories behind them like trolleys filled with emotional luggage. And of course, there are those thoughts that come in groups, whispering, gossiping, and causing trouble.

This constant traffic explains why people feel mentally tired even on days when they physically do nothing. The brain is running a 24-hour reception desk inside a bathroom open to the universe.

Not All Thoughts Should Be Treated Equally

In the mind's bathroom, thoughts queue up based on emotional urgency rather than importance. This is why something trivial feels huge while something serious goes unnoticed. A thought about an embarrassing moment from three years ago will push its way to the front of the line, while a thought about your life goals quietly stands in the corner waiting for its turn.

Humans often treat every thought like a VIP. But the truth is:

Some thoughts deserve attention.
Most thoughts deserve observation.
Very few thoughts deserve a long stay.

But because people never learn how to filter, they end up giving their mental front-row seats to thoughts that don't deserve chairs at all.

Imagine your mind as a waiting room where:

- The loudest thoughts get the most attention
- The oldest memories refuse to leave
- The newest fears act like emergencies
- The smallest worries behave like tragedies
- The simplest ideas wait patiently until you're relaxed enough to hear them

This is not dysfunction.
This is human nature.

Why Thoughts Don't Leave Until You Acknowledge Them

The mind is not a dictator. It does not delete thoughts by force. Instead, it works on recognition. Thoughts leave when they feel seen. Ignored thoughts don't vanish; they simply get louder. They repeat themselves, loop themselves, and sometimes wear disguises to sneak back in.

This is why suppressed emotions return as anxiety.
Why unresolved memories return as intrusive thoughts.
Why worries return every night at 2 a.m.
Why anger returns in small irritations.
Why fear returns as hesitation.

The mind's bathroom has one rule:
What you refuse to face, you are forced to feel.

Acknowledgment is the flush mechanism of the psyche.
Not analysis.
Not avoidance.
Not denial.
Just acknowledgment.

Overcrowding Happens When You Don't Let Thoughts Flow

The mind's bathroom is designed to handle a natural flow of thoughts much like water flowing through a pipe. But when you block the flow, thoughts pile up quickly.

Here's what overcrowding looks like:

- You overreact to small situations
- Your stress feels disproportionate
- You feel mentally cluttered
- Your attention becomes fragmented
- You cannot rest even when you're free
- Your inner dialogue becomes noisy
- You feel the need to constantly distract yourself

This is not because life is overwhelming it is because the mind's bathroom is overcrowded with unprocessed thoughts still waiting in line.

The problem is rarely the size of the thought; it is the number of thoughts you still haven't released.

Some Thoughts Are Simply Passing Through

One of the biggest misunderstandings in human psychology is the belief that every thought must mean something. In reality, most thoughts are like visitors who came to the wrong address.

Some thoughts arrive by accident.
Some are leftovers from yesterday.
Some are echoes of conversations.
Some are fears rehearsing for nothing.
Some are fantasies trying to entertain you.
Some are emotional weather patterns passing through.

You don't need to analyze every thought.
You don't need to fight every thought.
You don't need to fix every thought.

Most of them are just passing through, waiting for you to stop grabbing them so they can continue their journey.

The Bathroom Becomes Peaceful When You Stop Arguing With Thoughts

Thoughts are like people in line: they become louder when they feel ignored or resisted. The more you argue with a thought:

- "Why am I feeling this?"
- "I shouldn't think this."
- "This is wrong."
- "This means something bad."

... the more the thought takes this as an invitation to stay longer.

Arguing with thoughts is like arguing with someone in a public bathroom it only draws more attention to the situation.

The key to peace is simple:
Observe the thought without inviting it to a tea party.

A peaceful mind is not an empty mind it is a mind where thoughts come and go without drama.

Humor Makes the Bathroom Less Scary

If you can laugh at your thoughts, you can tame them. Humor is the oxygen of the mind's bathroom. It:

- Reduces emotional charge
- Breaks cognitive rigidity
- Softens self-judgment
- Balances perspective
- Releases mental tension

Humor turns the mind from a battlefield into a playground. When you laugh at your inner chaos, the chaos becomes a story not a threat.

Laughing at your thoughts doesn't belittle them; it liberates you.

The Bathroom Is Only Scary When the Light Is Off

Most people are afraid of their thoughts because they look at them in the dark when they're tired, stressed, unsure, or overworked. In the dark, every shadow looks bigger, every sound feels threatening, and every memory becomes dramatic.

Turn on the light awareness, humor, perspective and the bathroom becomes just another room.

A mind illuminated by awareness becomes peaceful even when full.
A mind in darkness becomes overwhelmed even when empty.

Your thoughts are not the enemy.
Your lack of light is.

The Bathroom Will Never Close But It Can Stay Uncrowded

You cannot stop thoughts from entering.
You should not stop thoughts from entering.
The mind was designed to think, not to stay silent.

Your power lies in:

- What you choose to keep
- What you choose to release
- What you choose to ignore
- What you choose to learn from
- What you choose to let pass

Thoughts are not meant to be stored.
They are meant to flow.

When you allow the flow, the mind's bathroom becomes peaceful a place of clarity, not chaos.

"The mind becomes calm not when thoughts stop arriving, but when you stop giving every thought a reason to stay."

CHAPTER 7 Letting Go Before You Burst

The Art of Release: Why Your Peace Depends on What You Stop Holding, Not What You Keep

There comes a moment in everyone's life several times a day, actually when the internal pressure becomes impossible to ignore. Something tightens inside you. A restlessness crawls beneath your ribs. Your mind begins pacing like a frustrated customer waiting for service. The tension rises, and your entire being whispers one simple truth: **"You need to let this go."**

But instead of letting go, most people do what humans are famously skilled at: **they hold, hold, and hold some more.** They grip their emotions. They grip their regrets. They grip their fears. They grip their imagined disasters. They grip arguments that ended last week. They grip versions of themselves that no longer exist. And they grip the expectation that if they hold long enough, the problem will magically resolve itself.

Spoiler: it won't.
Holding creates pressure.
Pressure creates discomfort.
Discomfort creates suffering.
Suffering creates confusion.
Confusion creates more thoughts.
And more thoughts create... more things to hold.

This is how people end up bursting in unexpected ways sudden anger, unexpected sadness, random anxiety, emotional shutdown, or mental exhaustion. Not because life is too heavy, but because they've been carrying far more than they were designed to carry.

Letting go isn't a luxury.
It's **maintenance**.

The Human Obsession With Holding Everything In

No animal in the world holds emotional waste the way humans do. A lion doesn't overthink past mistakes. A bird doesn't rehearse future disasters. A deer doesn't stay awake at midnight worrying about the next morning's predators. They experience life, respond, and release.

Humans, however, collect everything every comment, every look, every disappointment, every insecurity, every fear, every mistake, every "what if," every "I should have," every imagined future scenario. If the mind were a physical room, it would look like the garage of someone who never throws anything away because "it might be useful someday."

But here's the truth:
Most of what you hold is not useful.
Most of it is emotional clutter disguised as important information.

People hold because they believe holding protects them.
But holding only hurts them.

Letting Go Is Not Forgetting It Is Unclenching

Letting go is not pretending something never happened. It is not ignoring your experiences. It is not suppressing your feelings. Letting go is simply this:

Stop gripping the memory, emotion, or thought that is gripping your peace.

When the mind grips something tightly, the body joins in. Muscles tense. Breathing shortens. The chest feels heavy. The jaw stiffens. Even the stomach becomes sensitive. This is your entire system saying:

"You are holding something that must be released."

The moment you unclench physically and mentally space appears. Clarity appears. Perspective returns. Letting go is not an erasing process; it is a releasing one. You're not eliminating the past; you're stopping it from strangling the present.

Why People Wait Until They Burst

People don't hold because they're flawed. They hold because they're afraid.

They fear the emotional mess of releasing.
They fear the vulnerability of being honest with themselves.
They fear the uncertainty of facing the truth.
They fear losing a version of themselves built on old

stories.
They fear that letting go means losing control.

But bursting is the real loss of control.

Letting go is the *prevention*. Bursting is the *result* of refusing that prevention.

Think of a balloon. It doesn't burst because someone poked it. It bursts because the pressure inside became greater than what the structure could hold. Humans are the same.

You burst because you waited too long to release.

Release Is a Skill, Not an Accident

Most people think letting go is something that happens spontaneously during a breakdown, during a deep conversation, or after an emotional overload. But true release is a *skill* that can be learned.

Here are the four steps of emotional release:

1. Awareness: "I am holding something heavy."

Half of healing is recognizing the weight.
Holding is unconscious; letting go is conscious.

2. Acknowledgment: "This feeling is valid."

Feelings ask for recognition, not explanation.
When you validate them, they soften automatically.

3. Non-attachment: "This feeling is not me."

You are the sky; emotions are the weather.
You observe them; you don't become them.

4. Release: "It can go now."

Release happens in the moment you stop arguing with the emotion
and stop trying to "fix" it with thoughts.

Release is surrender, not defeat.
It is acceptance, not avoidance.
It is wisdom, not weakness.

Why Letting Go Feels Physically Lighter

When you let go, the change is not only psychological it is biological. The body relaxes as soon as the mind stops gripping.

- Shoulders drop
- The jaw releases
- Breathing deepens
- Heart rate stabilizes
- Tension dissolves
- The stomach loosens
- Vision softens
- Thoughts quiet down

Your entire system recognizes release as safety.

Letting go is not a thought.
Letting go is a physical experience.

Pressure lives in the body.
Release happens in the body.
Freedom is felt in the body.

Which Thoughts Need Release?

Not every thought is toxic. Not every feeling needs to be cleansed. But some are unmistakable candidates for release:

- The conversations you keep replaying
- The regrets you cannot change
- The people who no longer belong in your future
- The fears that are not based on truth
- The expectations that exhaust you
- The guilt that has already taught its lesson
- The version of yourself you've outgrown
- The memories that drain your energy
- The anger that has become stale
- The "what ifs" that paralyze your possibilities

These thoughts do not need solving.
They need releasing.

Life Changes When You Learn to Release Early

When you stop holding everything in, you stop living in survival mode. You begin to respond instead of react. You begin to see instead of fear. You begin to choose instead of endure.

Release gives you:

- Mental clarity
- Emotional stability
- Spiritual peace
- Creative freedom
- Psychological flexibility
- Physical relaxation
- A sense of inner spaciousness

Letting go early prevents the burst.
Letting go gently prevents the breakdown.
Letting go consistently prevents the chaos.

Release is not an end.
Release is a beginning.

The Peace on the Other Side of Letting Go

Imagine a life where nothing sits too long inside you.
Where thoughts come, teach, and leave.
Where emotions rise, express, and dissolve.
Where memories visit without hijacking your present.
Where fears whisper without controlling your steps.
Where expectations loosen their grip.
Where the past loses its authority.
Where the future loses its power to frighten you.

This is not fantasy.
This is what happens when you let go before you burst.

The mind becomes spacious.
The heart becomes soft.
The body becomes calm.
The spirit becomes light.

Letting go is not the end of caring.
It is the end of unnecessary suffering.

---

*"Letting go is not losing it is freeing the space
where your peace was meant to live."*

CHAPTER 8 The Freedom of Emptying the Mind

How a Lighter Brain Creates a Lighter Life (And Why Clarity Feels Better Than Intelligence)

There is a moment rare, precious, almost sacred when the mind becomes quiet enough for you to truly hear yourself. The noise fades. The internal chatter softens. The endless commentary pauses. And for a brief second, you feel something extraordinary: **space**. A spacious mind is not empty because it lacks thought; it is empty because it lacks *burden*. It is not hollow; it is free. It is not silent; it is peaceful.

This state is not an accident. It is the natural condition of a mind that knows how to release instead of retain, how to observe instead of overthink, and how to flow instead of freeze.

But most humans don't experience this condition consistently because the mind rarely gets the chance to empty. We don't give it the silence it needs. We don't give it stillness. We don't give it breathing room. Instead, we keep feeding it news, messages, fears, comparisons, stimulation, analysis, arguments, goals, expectations, pressure, opinions, and the heavy weight of tomorrow's responsibilities.

The modern world has trained the mind to stay full.
But wisdom begins when you learn the art of **emptying**.

The Myth: "A Busy Mind Is a Productive Mind"

Society loves busyness. It treats mental overload like a badge of honor. People brag about how exhausted they are, as if exhaustion proves anything other than mismanagement of their inner world. A busy mind is not a sign of intelligence it is a sign of congestion.

Intelligence is the ability to think.
Wisdom is the ability to stop thinking when necessary.

The truth is simple:
A full mind cannot see clearly.
A full mind cannot feel lightly.
A full mind cannot choose wisely.

No matter how smart you are, no matter how experienced, no matter how ambitious if your mind is too full, you will struggle to make even the simplest decisions. Fullness creates fog. Fog creates confusion. Confusion creates anxiety. Anxiety creates more thoughts. And suddenly, your mental life becomes a traffic jam with no exit.

Emptying the mind is not laziness; it is maintenance.
It is clarity.
It is discipline.
It is strength.

Why the Mind Loves to Hoard Thoughts

If the mind had a personality, it would be a combination of a librarian, a detective, and a paranoid squirrel. It collects information, stores memories, connects unrelated patterns, and hides emotional nuts in random corners "just in case" you need them later.

This hoarding behavior comes from three main instincts:

1. The Survival Instinct

The mind thinks keeping every thought will keep you safe.
It believes rehearsing danger will prevent danger.

2. The Ego Instinct

The mind believes more thinking will make you more in control, more certain, more important.
It equates thought with identity.

3. The Emotional Instinct

The mind tries to protect you by holding memories that once hurt you, hoping to prevent future pain.

But none of these instincts help.
They only add weight.

The mind is not supposed to store everything.
It is supposed to **filter**.

Emptying the Mind Is Not Forgetting It Is Unburdening

Many people fear the idea of an empty mind. They imagine becoming careless, emotionless, or unproductive. But emptying the mind does not remove intelligence. It removes noise.

Think of the mind like a glass of water. If the water is muddy, you cannot see through it. But when the sediment settles when the mind empties clarity emerges naturally. Emptying is not erasing. It is allowing the noise to settle so the truth can rise.

You do not lose anything by emptying the mind. You gain everything the noise was hiding.

The Three Layers of Mental Emptying

Emptying the mind happens in layers slowly, gently, intentionally.

Layer 1 Surface Emptying: Quieting the Immediate Noise

These are the random thoughts that jump around:
"What should I eat?"
"Did I forget something?"
"What if I just embarrass myself later?"
"What's the weather?"
"Why hasn't that person replied?"

This layer clears with short pauses, deep breaths, silence, or stepping away from stimulation. It is the mind exhaling.

Layer 2   Emotional Emptying: Releasing Stored Feelings

This layer is deeper. It includes:
Unprocessed sadness
Silent anger
Lingering guilt
Old fears
Internal pressure

This layer empties when you allow emotions to move through you without resistance. Crying, laughing, journaling, talking, reflecting, or simply acknowledging the feeling releases this layer.

Layer 3   Identity Emptying: Letting Go of the Roles You Force on Yourself

This is the deepest layer. It involves letting go of:

- The version of yourself you're trying to protect
- The expectations of who you "should" be
- The pressure to be perfect
- The masks you wear for society
- The fears connected to identity

When this layer empties, you don't just feel lighter you feel reborn.

Freedom on the Other Side of Emptying

A mind that knows how to empty becomes a powerful instrument:

1. Decisions Become Clear
    a. You no longer debate endlessly.
       You simply know.
2. Emotions Become Natural
    a. You feel without drowning.
       You release without fearing.
3. Relationships Become Authentic
    a. You stop reacting from baggage.
       You start responding from presence.
4. Creativity Increases
    a. A clear mind has space for new ideas.
       A full mind only recycles old ones.
5. Anxiety Reduces
    a. Most anxiety comes from mental overcrowding.
       Emptying dissolves this pressure.
6. Life Becomes Simpler
    a. Not because life changes,
       but because perception changes.
7. Peace Becomes Accessible
    a. Peace is not found through control
       peace is found through release.

An empty mind is not the absence of thought.
It is the presence of freedom.

The Mind Empties When You Stop Holding Everything

You empty your mind by releasing:

- Old stories you keep replaying
- Unnecessary analysis
- Thoughts that don't serve your growth
- Senseless worries
- Emotional leftovers
- Mental habits that exhaust you
- Future projections you can't control
- Past regrets that no longer teach anything

You empty your mind by **unburdening** it.

Just as the body sighs when relieved,
the mind sighs when emptied.

Silence becomes sweet.
Stillness becomes comforting.
Life becomes spacious.

Humor Helps the Mind Empty Naturally

A funny thing happens when you laugh: your mind drops everything for a moment. Humor pulls you into the present so strongly that thoughts lose their grip. Laughter is the mind emptying itself without effort.

This is why the wisest people have a sense of humor. Humor is not a personality trait it is a mental cleansing tool.

A mind that laughs empties.
A mind that empties sees.
A mind that sees lives fully.

Emptying the Mind Is Not Escaping Life It Is Experiencing Life

When the mind is full, you live through a filter of noise. When the mind empties, you live through a window of clarity.

Emptying the mind does not separate you from reality. It connects you to it.

You notice beauty.
You notice silence.
You notice breath.
You notice yourself.

And for the first time in a long time,
you feel alive without effort.

"A mind is never truly free until it learns the art of releasing what it does not need to think."

CHAPTER 9 Flush the Past: Clearing What No Longer Serves You

Why Yesterday Doesn't Deserve Unlimited Storage in Your Mind

There comes a time in every person's life when they must face a difficult truth: **the past does not leave until you release it**. It stays inside you, not as history, but as unfinished business. Every memory you didn't fully process, every wound you pretended wasn't deep, every moment you replay instead of resolving all of it becomes emotional residue. And just like physical residue, it clogs the system. It slows the mind. It thickens the heart. It muddies clarity. It steals energy. The past becomes heavy not because it is large, but because **you keep carrying pieces you were never meant to keep**.

This chapter is about flushing the things that no longer belong in the present memories, regrets, beliefs, grudges, comparisons, conversations, identities, expectations, and especially old versions of yourself that no longer fit who you are becoming.

Flushing is not forgetting.
Flushing is **freeing**.

Freeing the mind from emotional sediment.
Freeing the heart from psychological weight.
Freeing your future from the fingerprints of yesterday.

Why the Past Holds So Much Power

The past is persuasive. It whispers gently at first reminding you of successes, failures, lessons, hurts, mistakes, loves, and losses. But when the past feels threatened, it speaks louder. Memories gain sharp edges. Old emotions return with urgency. Forgotten stories rise from the depths as if demanding attention.

The past's power comes from three illusions:

1. **"The past defines who I am."**

    People cling to identity even when it's painful.
    "I am this way because of what happened."
    But identity is a choice, not a prison.

2. **"If I let go, I will lose the lesson."**

    Lessons don't need pain to remain.
    Wisdom stays even after the suffering ends.

3. **"Holding on keeps me safe."**

    No.
    Holding on keeps you stuck.
    Flushing keeps you safe.

The past holds power only when you hold it back.

Memories You Keep Are Not Always Memories That Help You

Not all memories are useful. Some are outdated files that no longer serve your growth.

People tend to store:

- The moments that embarrassed them
- The words that wounded them
- The mistakes they regret
- The love they lost
- The opportunities they missed
- The people who disappointed them
- The fears that once protected them
- The failures that shaped their self-worth

These memories sit in the mind like unpaid bills demanding attention long after their purpose has expired.

You do not grow by remembering the pain.
You grow by understanding the lesson and releasing the suffering.

The Danger of Unflushed Emotions

Old emotions are like stagnant water, they become cloudy, heavy, and eventually toxic. What you don't release, you relive. This is why you suddenly feel sad for "no reason," angry at something small, or vulnerable without explanation.

The past leaks into the present through emotional pressure.

- A past rejection makes you fear new opportunities.
- A past betrayal makes you mistrust kind people.
- A past mistake makes you hesitant to try again.
- A past heartbreak makes you hide your heart.

- A past embarrassment makes you hyper-aware of yourself.

These ghosts of the past act like invisible walls between you and the life you want.

But the truth is simple:
You are not avoiding danger, you're avoiding freedom.

Your Mind Has a Limited Capacity

Imagine if your phone kept every notification, message, photo, file, and update since the day you bought it. It would freeze. It would slow down. It would become unusable.

Humans do the same with emotional and mental content. The mind becomes sluggish not because life is overwhelming, but because **the past is overloading the present.**

A full past leaves no room for a new future.

Just as your phone needs a regular cleanup, your mind needs regular emotional clearing. The past must be flushed to create space for the next version of your life.

Why People Resist Flushing

People avoid flushing the past because of emotional investment. They believe:

- If I let go, I will lose part of myself.

- If I release this memory, its meaning will disappear.
- If I stop replying to this moment, I will repeat the mistake.
- If I forgive, the other person wins.

But none of this is true.

Flushing the past is not betrayal.
It is liberation.

It does not erase meaning.
It erases suffering.

It does not remove wisdom.
It removes weight.

It does not help the other person.
It helps **you**.

The past is not a museum to preserve.
It is a toolbox to use when needed and then close.

Letting the Past Flow Instead of Flood

A healthy mind doesn't hold the past.
A healthy mind allows the past to flow.

Here's the difference:

- **Holding:**
  "Why did this happen? Why me? What if...? What if not...?"
  This leads to rumination.

- **Flowing:**
  "It happened. I learned. I release."
  This leads to peace.

Flow is not passive.
Flow is wise.

It is the choice to stop wrestling with what cannot change and start focusing on what can.

The Mind Flushes Through Understanding, Not Suppression

People mistakenly believe that flushing means *forgetting* or *ignoring*.
But suppression is not flushing.
Suppression is stuffing.

Real flushing requires consciousness:

1. See the memory honestly.
2. Feel the emotion without judgment.
3. Extract the lesson.
4. Release the emotional charge.
5. Let the memory return to silence.

The event will remain in your history,
but it will no longer run your present.

Forgiveness Is Not a Gift to Others It Is Emotional Plumbing

Forgiveness is nothing mystical.
It is plumbing.
It unclogs the emotional pipe so your peace can flow again.

Forgiveness is not approval.
Forgiveness is not forgetting.
Forgiveness is not reconciliation.
Forgiveness is not trust.

Forgiveness is **decluttering your own heart.**
It is saying:
"I refuse to carry this anymore. This is not my weight."

Forgiveness flushes the emotional residue the past left behind.

The Past Cannot Hurt You Only Your Attachment to It Can

The past is powerless.
It cannot reach into the present unless you keep opening the door.

Pain from the past is not from the event it is from your grip.
The moment you loosen that grip; the past loses authority.

People say, "time heals," but actually:

Release heals.
Acceptance heals.
Understanding heals.

Detachment heals.
Flush heals.

Time only passes.

Healing happens when you empty the emotional tank.

Your Future Depends on What You Flush Today

Your next chapter cannot begin while your previous chapters are still scattered across your inner world. The mind needs space to imagine, create, connect, grow, and choose.

When you flush the past:

- You reclaim energy.
- You regain clarity.
- You reopen possibilities.
- You rebuild self-trust.
- You rediscover joy.
- You rewrite your identity.

A light future requires a light heart.
A light heart requires a flushed past.

Your life expands when your mind empties.

"You cannot step into your future with the footprints of your past still inside your mind."

CHAPTER 10 The Bathroom of Enlightenment

Why Your Deepest Thoughts Arrive When You're Alone with Your Silence (And Sometimes, Your Plumbing)

There is something universally human, wildly consistent, and oddly profound about the moments when clarity strikes. You're sitting alone, away from people, away from noise, away from responsibility, just you, your thoughts, and the unmistakable echo of solitude. Then suddenly, out of nowhere, wisdom appears. Not because you forced it. Not because you tried. But because **silence made enough room for truth to enter.**

It is no coincidence that some of humanity's greatest insights have arrived in the shower, on a quiet walk, lying in bed before sleep, or let's be honest during a peaceful bathroom break. Philosophers meditate for hours to achieve what many people accidentally discover every morning when they are left undisturbed: **the mind reveals its wisdom when the world stops demanding its attention.**

This chapter explores an ancient, humorous truth: **your most enlightened moments often happen in the least glamorous places.** Not because the environment is sacred, but because your mind is finally unburdened enough to think clearly.

Enlightenment is not location-dependent.
It is attention-dependent.

The Most Private Room Is Also the Most Honest Room

The bathroom is one of the very few places in the modern world where humans cannot pretend. You cannot perform a role there. You cannot act like someone else. You cannot multitask. You cannot negotiate with your identity. You cannot entertain an audience. You cannot hide behind your title, your job, your status, your responsibilities, or your ego.

In the bathroom, **every person on Earth becomes equal.**
Kings are equal to janitors.
Celebrities are equal to students.
Millionaires are equal to monks.
The powerful, the humble, the anxious, the confident everyone shares the same biological truth.

It is the one place where the external world stops and the internal world begins. And it is often the first place where the mind whispers what it has been trying to say all day.

In that quiet room, you are no longer performing life.
You are simply *being*.

And in being, wisdom finds space.

Clarity Comes When the Mind Stops Competing with Noise

The mind is like a lake. When disturbed by wind, waves distort the reflections. But when the wind stops, even for a moment, the water becomes still enough to reflect the sky. That stillness is what you experience during quiet, solitary moments especially in places where nobody expects anything from you.

The reason your best ideas appear during:

- long showers
- isolated walks
- late-night bathroom trips
- quiet moments before sleep
- and yes, while sitting peacefully on the toilet

... is because these are the rare moments when **your mind is no longer fighting external demands.**

Your brain gets a break.
Your nervous system softens.
Your thinking slows down.
Your awareness sharpens.

And in this space, ideas rise. Insights surface. Solutions unfold.

The bathroom is not magical
stillness is.

Why Enlightenment Feels So Accidental

Most people don't aim for enlightenment. They stumble into it. It hits them mid-shower:
"Oh! That's what I should do!"

Or during a quiet moment alone:
"Now I understand why that happened."

Or while sitting calmly with nothing to distract them:
"I finally see the truth."

The insight feels accidental because **you didn't create the idea you created the conditions for the idea to appear.**

Enlightenment is the absence of interference.

Wisdom doesn't need pushing; it needs space.
Solutions don't need pressure; they need clarity.
Insight doesn't need effort; it needs stillness.

Most minds stay too occupied to receive their own intelligence.

The Bathroom Teaches a Spiritual Lesson: Release Leads to Realization

There is something psychologically poetic about what happens in the bathroom:
You release what the body no longer needs.
You release pressure.
You release tension.
You release discomfort.

And as the body releases, so does the mind.

Physical release creates mental openness.
This is why so many people walk out of the bathroom feeling lighter in more ways than one.

Release empties you.
Emptiness creates space.
Space allows clarity to enter.
Clarity creates realization.
Realization becomes enlightenment.

It is not the bathroom it is the act of release.

You cannot receive insight while holding everything inside.
The universe speaks when your mind stops gripping.

Humor Makes Enlightenment Accessible

Spiritual teachers across centuries spoke about enlightenment as if it were a precious gemstone hidden on a mountaintop. But the truth is much simpler: enlightenment arrives in ordinary moments when the mind is quiet enough to notice life's obvious truths.

Humor makes these truths easier to understand.
The bathroom becomes a metaphor:
A place where nothing pretentious survives.
A place where you are just human.
A place where ego dissolves instantly.
A place where the mind finally breathes.

When you laugh at your own human nature, you create the humility required for real insight. Humor softens the walls of the mind. And when the walls soften, wisdom enters like sunlight through an open window.

A person who takes themselves too seriously cannot see clearly.
A person who understands their own ridiculousness becomes wise.

Solitude Is the Teacher, Stillness Is the Classroom

The bathroom is simply one of the few remaining spaces of guaranteed solitude. Solitude calms the mind. Stillness organizes thoughts. Silence amplifies understanding.

In solitude, you meet yourself.
In stillness, you hear yourself.
In silence, you understand yourself.

This is why bathrooms, showers, meditation rooms, long walks, and moments of isolation all produce the same results: insight.

Enlightenment is not a ceremony.
It is not a ritual.
It is not a mystical achievement.
It is the natural consequence of an unburdened mind.

And every person, no matter what their background, experiences these micro-enlightenments daily if they allow themselves to stop and listen.

Enlightenment Is Not a Peak It Is a Pause

Most people imagine enlightenment as a dramatic moment: a mountain summit, a cosmic vision, a life-changing realization. But the truth is far humbler and far more accessible.

Enlightenment is not a peak experience.
It is a pause experience.

A pause in thought.
A pause in pressure.
A pause in identity.
A pause in fear.
A pause in the need to control.

In that pause, the mind aligns with truth.

You don't climb to enlightenment.
You relax into it.

The Bathroom Is a Symbol of What the Mind Needs Daily

Quiet.
Privacy.
Safety.
Stillness.
Release.

When the mind receives these ingredients, it becomes spacious enough to produce wisdom without force.

If you give your mind a bathroom-level break once a day it will repay you with clarity, peace, and insight far greater than anything produced through stress or effort.

A relaxed mind is an enlightened mind.
A burdened mind is a noisy mind.
Noise hides wisdom.
Space reveals it.

"Enlightenment rarely arrives with effort it appears in the moments you finally give your mind a place to breathe."

CHAPTER 11   Philosophers, Sufis & Zen Masters: Masters of the Mental Pee

Why the Wisest Minds in History Were Experts in Release, Flow, and Emptying the Inner Tank

Across centuries, the world has admired philosophers, mystics, poets, Zen masters, Stoics, monks, and sages for their ability to remain calm in chaos, wise in confusion, and peaceful in pressure. We think they possessed supernatural abilities divine visions, cosmic secrets, elevated intellects, extraordinary discipline. But in reality, these great minds shared one simple skill:

They knew how to empty their mental tank before it overflowed.

Their entire philosophy revolved around release letting go of unnecessary thoughts, dissolving ego, surrendering illusions, and living in flow rather than friction. They mastered the art of not gripping what didn't belong inside them. They knew that wisdom doesn't come from thinking more it comes from thinking *clearly*. And clarity is impossible without flow.

This chapter will reveal a humorous and surprisingly accurate truth:
history's greatest spiritual and philosophical teachers

were basically early experts in "mental peeing."
Not literal, of course, but psychological. They released everything the mind didn't need, long before modern psychology discovered the benefit.

Their teachings echo one message across cultures:
Empty your mind and wisdom enters. Hold everything inside and suffering grows.

Why Ancient Thinkers Focused on Emptiness Instead of Accumulation

In today's world, everyone wants to *accumulate*: knowledge, opinions, information, achievements, prestige, followers, validation. But ancient masters were smarter they knew that accumulating too much, mentally or emotionally, makes life heavier.

The Stoics taught detachment.

They said:
"Control what you can, release what you can't."
Or in modern language:
"Stop holding things you cannot flush."

The Sufis taught surrender.

They said:
"Empty yourself of everything that is not love."
Translation:
"Remove the emotional junk blocking your peace."

The Zen masters taught no-mind (mushin).

They said:
"When the mind is empty, everything becomes possible."
Or more humorously:
"Let thoughts pass like clouds, not like furniture."

Buddha taught the middle path and non-attachment.

He said:
"Suffering arises from clinging."
Meaning:
"You are drowning not because life is deep, but because you're gripping the stones."

Across cultures, the message is identical:
Do not hold what is meant to pass.

Ancients understood flow long before we invented plumbing.

Sufis and the Beauty of Inner Release

Sufi mystics were masters of letting go. They believed the human heart becomes heavy not from experience but from *attachment*. They danced, sang, wrote poetry, and practiced stillness all to encourage the mind to drop whatever was blocking divine presence.

Rumi said:
"Why are you so busy with the world? Learn to release."
He didn't say "pee," but he meant "release unnecessary weight."

Sufis believed that when you empty your inner tank of ego, fear, judgment, and overthinking, **your soul becomes spacious enough to experience truth directly.**

Their practice was not about thinking deeply it was about thinking lightly.

A heart free of clutter becomes a mirror.
A mind free of clutter becomes a window.

Zen Masters and the Art of Flow

Zen masters understood one thing better than anyone else:
The mind becomes wise when it stops gripping reality.

They trained students to sit in silence, allowing thoughts to come and go without attachment. If the thought stayed, fine. If it left, fine. If it looped, fine. Nothing was personal.

Zen masters often answered questions with cryptic humor:

Student:
"Master, how do I achieve enlightenment?"

Master:
"When hungry, eat. When tired, sleep."

Student:
"What does that have to do with wisdom?"

Master:
"You overcomplicate your own existence."

Zen is brutal simplicity.
It's the philosophy of flow.
It teaches that the mind becomes peaceful not by adding more but by removing excess.

Zen is the spiritual version of letting pee flow naturally:
Don't force.
Don't hold.
Don't panic.
Just allow.

Stoics and the Emotional Plumbing System

The Stoics were ancient emotional plumbers. They taught people how to maintain internal peace by stopping emotional overflow.

Seneca said:
"We suffer more in imagination than in reality."
Translation:
"Your mind's toilet is clogged with imaginary fears flush them."

Marcus Aurelius said:
"You have power over your mind, not outside events."
In modern language:
"Control what thoughts you admit into your bathroom."

Epictetus said:
"It's not things that disturb us, but our opinions about them."
Meaning:

"You're upset not because of the situation but because you're holding it wrong."

Stoicism is practical enlightenment.
It teaches resilience by releasing emotional pressure early.

They didn't suppress emotion.
They understood emotion.
Then they let it go.

Ancient Greek Philosophers: Masters of Thought, Not Thought-Hoarding

Plato, Aristotle, Socrates they engaged with ideas deeply, but they didn't hold onto every idea. They questioned thoughts. They examined them. They challenged them. But they did not drown in them.

Socrates famously said:
"I know that I know nothing."
This wasn't humility it was mental clarity.
He flushed his own certainty to make room for truth.

Most modern overthinkers would benefit from this.
Instead of trying to store every thought, question each one:
"Do you belong here?"
"Are you useful?"
"Do you serve my peace or disturb it?"

Philosophers were thinkers, yes
but they were not thought-hoarders.

They practiced mental decluttering centuries before psychology did.

What All Masters Have in Common

Across cultures, across centuries, across spiritual traditions, every enlightened figure discovered the same principle:

The mind becomes wise through release, not retention.

They all mastered:

- Letting go
- Nonattachment
- Flow
- Surrender
- Stillness
- Awareness
- Inner emptiness
- Emotional release
- Ego softening
- Thought observation

They knew that a full mind is blind,
an empty mind sees.

They knew that holding too much blocks growth.
They knew that release is the doorway to transformation.

Simply put:

**Ancient masters didn't let thoughts pile up.
They let thoughts pass through.**

Why Modern People Suffer More Than Ancient Mystics

Because ancient mystics lived in silence.
Modern people live in noise.

Ancients lived slowly.
Modern people live hectically.

Ancients valued internal clarity.
Modern people value external accomplishment.

Ancients focused on flow.
Modern people focus on accumulation.

Ancients emptied their minds daily.
Modern people wait until they break down.

The mystics didn't escape life.
They mastered living lightly.

Modern suffering comes from this single difference:
We hold everything they learned to let go.

You Are Capable of the Same Peace

You don't need to become a monk.
You don't need to meditate in a cave.
You don't need to memorize scriptures.

You only need to practice what the wisest people mastered:

the art of releasing mental pressure before it becomes pain.

This is the real meaning of modern enlightenment: to become a master of your inner flow.

To know what to keep.
To know what to release.
To know when to stop thinking.
To know when to start living.

The wisdom of the masters is not out of reach.
It is already inside you
hidden behind the clutter you're still holding.

"The wisest people weren't those who thought more, but those who learned how to let their thoughts pass through without owning every one."

CHAPTER 12 Pressure Is Not the Enemy Avoidance Is

Why Life Doesn't Break You But Your Habit of Running From Your Inner Truth Might

Pressure is one of the most misunderstood forces in the human experience. People treat it like a villain something to fear, escape, silence, or avoid at all costs. But pressure is not the enemy. Pressure is a messenger. A teacher. A signal that something inside you needs movement. It is your mind, heart, and nervous system gently whispering, then urgently shouting:

"Please stop avoiding this. Face it. Release it. Let it flow."

If pressure were truly harmful, you would not feel relief after releasing it. Physically, emotionally, psychologically release always brings peace. It is not pressure that hurts you; it is the *resistance* to pressure. The clenching. The suppressing. The running. The avoidance. The stubborn belief that if you don't look at something, it will magically resolve itself.

Avoidance does not protect you.
Avoidance preserves the problem.

Avoidance is the invisible wall between you and peace.

Pressure Exists Because You Are Alive

Every living system creates pressure:
The lungs expand.
The heart pumps.
The stomach processes.
The mind thinks.
The emotions move.

Pressure is simply movement. Life. Flow.

The problem begins when you refuse to respond to pressure. When you try to silence a feeling. Ignore a thought. Hide from a truth. Avoid a conversation. Dismiss a memory. Delay a decision. Push away discomfort. Pretend you're fine when every part of you knows you're not.

Avoidance is the spiritual equivalent of covering your ears and saying "la-la-la" while standing in front of a fire alarm.

The alarm is not the problem.
The fire is.

Avoidance Pretends to Protect but Actually Traps You

When you avoid something, you think you're escaping it. In reality, you're wrapping chains around it and carrying it with you everywhere.

Avoidance says:
"I'm not ready to feel this."
"I don't want to think about this."
"This makes me uncomfortable."
"If I ignore it, it might go away."

But emotions don't leave just because you don't want to face them.
Thoughts don't vanish just because you choose distraction.
Unresolved truths don't dissolve just because you close your eyes.

Avoidance doesn't remove pressure.
Avoidance multiplies pressure.

You don't escape the weight, you internalize it.

Pressure Only Becomes Pain When It Has No Pathway Out

Pressure is not dangerous when it flows.
Pressure is dangerous when it gets trapped.

Think of your body:
If you drink water, pressure builds so you release it.
If you eat food, pressure builds so you digest it.
If you breathe, pressure builds so you exhale.

Nature designed everything to flow.
When flow stops, problems begin.

The same principle governs your inner life:

- Emotions are meant to move.
- Thoughts are meant to pass.
- Memories are meant to soften.
- Desires are meant to express.
- Truths are meant to be faced.

Avoidance blocks this natural flow.
And when flow stops, the mind becomes congested.

Pressure without movement becomes pain.
Pressure with movement becomes insight.

Avoidance Is a Fear of Feeling

Many people avoid not because they are weak, but because they are terrified of the emotions waiting on the other side of acknowledgment.

Avoidance is the fear of:

- sadness you tried to bury
- anger you're scared to express
- truth you're scared to accept
- change you don't feel ready for
- memories that still feel sharp
- decisions that feel overwhelming
- accountability that feels heavy

But here is the paradox:

Feeling the emotion is always less painful than carrying the emotion.

Avoidance is emotional interest you pay more the longer you delay.

The moment you actually face the feeling, it begins to dissolve.

Avoidance Keeps the Mind Full Pressure Helps Empty It

Pressure reminds you when something needs release.
Avoidance blocks release entirely.

Pressure says,
"Something inside wants space."
Avoidance says,
"Let's pretend we're fine."

Pressure asks for truth.
Avoidance asks for silence.

Pressure is the invitation to healing.
Avoidance is the postponement of healing.

People assume pressure means something is wrong.
In truth, pressure means something is **ready**.

Ready to be felt.
Ready to be released.
Ready to be understood.
Ready to be flushed.

Avoidance delays this readiness indefinitely.

The Emotional Cost of Avoiding Your Reality

Avoidance always shows up in subtle yet painful ways:

- Overthinking

- Anxiety
- Irritability
- Shallow breathing
- Restlessness
- Procrastination
- Emotional numbness
- Inability to relax
- Sensitivity to small triggers
- Sudden emotional outbursts
- Difficulty sleeping

These symptoms are not random.
They are the mind's desperate attempt to get you to face what you've been avoiding.

Avoidance is the reason many people feel emotionally tired even when nothing "big" is happening.
They're not exhausted from life.
They're exhausted from avoiding life.

Pressure Is a Teacher in Disguise

Pressure doesn't show up to break you it shows up to show you where you've stopped flowing.

Pressure teaches:

- where you're suppressing emotions
- where you're not being honest
- where you're resisting truth
- where you're afraid to act
- where you're carrying too much
- where you need to set a boundary
- where growth is waiting

Pressure points to the internal door you refuse to open.

Open it, and the pressure releases.
Avoid it, and the pressure multiplies.

The Strength You Seek Comes After Facing What You Fear

People often underestimate their emotional resilience.
They imagine that facing their inner truth will shatter them.
They believe confronting feelings will make them drown.

But reality is kinder:

**You don't drown when you face emotion.
You drown when you suppress emotion.**

The truth is always lighter than the fear of facing it.

Pressure becomes painful only when you resist it.
The moment you walk toward it, it becomes guidance.

Every time you face what you avoided, you reclaim a piece of your power.
Every time you release what was stuck, you expand.
Every time you flush the emotional tank, you grow.

Avoidance Breaks You Open Facing Yourself Breaks You Free

There is beauty in confronting your inner world.
It is not destruction; it is purification.
It is not defeat; it is awakening.

The more honest you become with yourself,
the lighter your life becomes.
The more you face,
the less you fear.
The less you hold,
the more you heal.

Avoidance prolongs suffering.
Connection with your truth dissolves it.

Pressure is simply life telling you:
"Something inside is ready to release.
Ready to flow.
Ready to evolve."

Avoidance is life whispering:
"You don't have to suffer.
You only have to see."

"Pressure doesn't break you resistance does. The moment you face what you've been avoiding, the weight lifts and the path opens."

CHAPTER 13 Think Light, Live Light

Why a Lighter Mind Creates a Lighter Life and How Simplicity Quietly Becomes the Ultimate Superpower

There is a moment in every person's journey when life begins to feel heavier than it should. The responsibilities pile up. The memories accumulate. The to-do lists expand. The comparisons increase. The worries multiply. The expectations tighten. And without noticing, the mind becomes weighed down by thoughts it never needed to keep in the first place.

Life wasn't designed to be this heavy.
We make it heavy by **overthinking what should be simple and holding what should be released**.
We complicate things that were meant to flow naturally.
We drag emotional baggage across years, even decades.
We carry old versions of ourselves into new chapters.
We hold fears that don't belong to our future.
We replay past mistakes as if they owe us answers.
We imagine worst-case scenarios as if fear were a fortune-teller.

But here's the truth the world often hides:
Your life becomes lighter the moment your thinking becomes lighter.

Thinking light does not mean thinking less.
It means thinking *cleanly*.
Thinking *freely*.
Thinking *without unnecessary weight*.
It means letting thoughts pass through instead of clinging to them like emotional souvenirs.

A light mind isn't empty
it is uncluttered.
It isn't detached
it is unburdened.
It isn't careless
it is compassionate with itself.

This chapter is about learning the art of thinking lightly, so you can begin living lightly.

The Heaviness You Feel Is Not Life It's Overthinking

Life itself is rarely as heavy as the stories we tell about it. The burden doesn't come from reality it comes from the narratives the mind attaches to reality.

Two people can face the same situation:
One feels crushed.
One feels challenged.

The difference is not the situation.
The difference is the mental weight.

Overthinking turns:

- a tiny inconvenience into a disaster

- a small uncertainty into fear
- a brief delay into rejection
- a simple conversation into a complex puzzle
- a normal mistake into a crisis of identity
- a passing problem into a permanent burden

Overthinking doesn't solve problems; it decorates them with fear.

A heavy mind creates a heavy world.

Light Thinking Begins With Discernment

A light mind is not a mind free of thoughts it is a mind free of unnecessary thoughts.
It knows how to ask:

- *Is this thought helpful?*
- *Is this fear realistic?*
- *Is this memory still relevant?*
- *Is this worry trying to protect me or punish me?*
- *Is this something I can control?*
- *Is this worth keeping?*

Heavy minds never ask these questions.
They accept every thought as truth.
They collect every emotion as permanent.
They store every memory as essential.
They treat every fear as prophecy.

Discernment is the filter that separates wisdom from noise.

Why Simplicity Is the Highest Form of Mental Intelligence

Anyone can complicate life.
Only the wise can simplify it.

Simplicity is not about reducing life it is about reducing friction.

It means:

- cutting unnecessary thoughts
- releasing old stories
- stopping mental rehearsals
- detaching from imagined catastrophes
- choosing clarity over chaos
- choosing presence over panic
- choosing acceptance over resistance

Simplicity is not the absence of depth.
Simplicity *is* depth refined, distilled, understood.

Think of the ocean.
On the surface, it moves wildly.
Deep inside, it is still.
That stillness is wisdom.

A light mind thinks from the depths, not the surface storms.

The Lighter the Thought, the Faster the Flow

Heavy thoughts stick.
They sit in your mind like furniture bulky, immovable, occupying space you didn't know you needed.

Light thoughts flow.
They move gently.
They pass through you without carving scars.

Heavy thoughts feel like:

- regret
- shame
- fear
- overanalysis
- comparison
- self-doubt
- resentment

Light thoughts feel like:

- acceptance
- curiosity
- possibility
- compassion
- awareness
- humor
- presence

Heavy thoughts push you into survival mode.
Light thoughts allow you to live.

Most of Life Does Not Require a Heavy Mind

The mind loves drama.
It loves to turn simple situations into emotional theatre.
It loves to add meaning to things that were meant to be neutral.
It loves to activate ancient fears in modern situations.

But most of life is simple:

- You wake.
- You feel.
- You act.
- You rest.
- You love.
- You lose.
- You learn.
- You continue.

The world complicates life.
Heavy thinking magnifies the complication.
Light thinking dissolves it.

What you lighten in your mind, you lighten in your world.

The Art of Thinking Lightly: A Practice, Not an Accident

You don't wake up one day suddenly thinking lightly.
You build it by practice.

Here are the principles:

1. Don't chase every thought

Most thoughts don't need attention they need permission to pass.

2. Don't interpret everything

Not every look, word, moment, or silence has a deep meaning.

3. Pause before taking things personally

People are carrying their own storms; most reactions aren't about you.

4. Reduce mental multitasking

A scattered mind becomes heavy.
Do one thing, think one thing, feel one thing at a time.

5. Humorize, don't dramatize

Life becomes lighter the moment you start laughing at your own intensity.

6. Let go sooner

The earlier you release, the lighter you remain.

7. Don't argue with reality

Acceptance is the heaviest weight remover.

8. Keep thoughts flowing

If a thought stays too long, it becomes a tenant.

Thinking lightly is not carelessness
it is care for your mental clarity.

Life Feels Easier When You Stop Holding Everything So Tightly

You are not meant to grip every emotion that passes through you.
You are not meant to worry about every possibility.
You are not meant to replay old mistakes like a painful movie.
You are not meant to analyze every detail of your existence.
You are not meant to judge yourself for every imperfection.

Life becomes easier when you:

- soften your grip
- reduce your intensity
- stop fighting your feelings
- stop resisting discomfort
- allow yourself to breathe
- allow yourself to be human
- allow mistakes without punishment

Lightness is not the absence of effort.
It is the presence of flow.

When your thinking becomes light, your life becomes spacious.
You stop drowning in details.

You start seeing the bigger picture.
You stop chasing problems.
You start living solutions.

The Destination of Light Thinking: Internal Freedom

When you think lightly, something incredible happens:

- You feel lighter in your chest.
- Your decisions become easier.
- Your relationships become softer.
- Your creativity expands.
- Your emotions move freely.
- Anxiety loses its grip.
- Peace becomes accessible.
- Presence becomes natural.
- Joy feels less accidental.

This is the freedom most people spend their lives chasing externally.

But freedom was never outside of you.
It was always in the way you think.

Light mind → Light heart → Light life.

"A heavy life begins in a heavy mind. When your thinking becomes light, the world follows."

CHAPTER 14   The Joy of Relief: Why Release Feels So Good

The Psychology, Biology, and Spiritual Magic Behind That "Ahhhh..." Moment of Letting Go

There is a universal human sound heard across cultures, languages, beliefs, ages, and continents that needs no translation. A sound produced not by words, but by relief. A long, gentle, involuntary exhale that escapes the body the moment pressure leaves it:

"Ahhhhh..."

That sound is the anthem of release.
The melody of a burden lifting.
The music of the mind remembering its natural state: freedom.

Whether you are finally releasing held-in tears, a long-kept truth, emotional tension, a stressful thought, or quite literally pee, the sensation is the same: **the body relaxes, the mind expands, the spirit softens, and the world suddenly feels lighter.**

Relief is not a luxury.
Relief is a biological celebration.
Relief is the mind, body, and soul aligning after letting go of something they were never meant to hold.

This chapter explores why relief feels so good and why humans are designed to experience joy, not through achievement, but through release.

Relief Is the Body's Reward for Letting Go

When you release physical pressure, your nervous system shifts instantly from a state of tension to a state of rest. Muscles unclench. Breathing deepens. Heart rate stabilizes. The brain releases endorphins the chemical cousins of happiness.

Your entire physiology celebrates release.

But this mechanism exists not just for the body it exists for the *mind*.

Emotional release triggers:

- dopamine (reward)
- oxytocin (trust and comfort)
- serotonin (well-being)
- endorphins (euphoria and relief)

This is why crying feels good, even when it comes from pain.
This is why telling the truth feels freeing, even when it's difficult.
This is why admitting your fear calms your fear.
This is why expressing your feelings makes you feel human again.
This is why releasing guilt creates peace.

This is why forgiveness feels like removing a heavy backpack.

Your biology rewards you for letting go.

Relief is the body's way of saying:
"Thank you for setting me free from what I could no longer carry."

Relief Is the Mind's Way of Returning to Balance

The mind is constantly managing incoming stimuli: thoughts, emotions, memories, stressors, expectations, responsibilities.
When you hold too much, the mind loses its elasticity.
It becomes rigid, overwhelmed, confused.

Release resets that elasticity.

Think of your mind as a bowstring.
If held tightly for too long, it loses flexibility.
But with release, it returns to its natural shape.

This is why:

- after a long cry, you think clearly
- after a deep talk, you feel lighter
- after telling someone the truth, your chest loosens
- after expressing anger, the mind quiets
- after forgiving someone, you feel spacious inside
- after letting go of a memory, your future feels brighter
- after surrendering a fear, your courage increases

Relief is the mind's homecoming.
Its way of saying:
"I am finally me again."

Relief Gives You Back Your Energy

Holding anything thoughts, emotions, grudges, fears consumes energy.
Not just emotional energy, but physical energy too.

That is why people feel:

- tired from overthinking
- exhausted from pretending
- drained from carrying old pain
- depleted from unresolved conflicts
- heavy from guilt or shame
- tense from unexpressed emotions

Release returns this energy to you.

Imagine carrying a heavy suitcase for ten miles.
The moment you drop it, the ground feels softer.
Your spine feels longer.
Your breath becomes more available.
The world becomes lighter.

This is what happens internally when you release emotional weight.
You are not getting stronger
you are removing what was weakening you.

Relief Is a Spiritual Reset

Every spiritual tradition honors the concept of release.

In Sufism:

"Open your hands what you cling to is what binds you."

In Buddhism:

"Suffering ends when clinging ends."

In Zen:

"Let go, or be dragged."

In Stoicism:

"Release what is not yours to control."

In Christianity:

"Cast your burdens."

In Hinduism:

"Surrender the fruits of your actions."

The message is identical:
Freedom is found not in accumulation, but in release.

Spiritual liberation is simply emotional unclenching.

Relief is a small awakening
a moment when the soul recognizes itself beneath the noise.

In that instant, you remember who you are before anxiety, before fear, before pressure, before expectation.

Relief is the mind bowing to the truth:
"I am meant to flow, not suffocate."

Relief Makes Space for Better Things to Enter

When you hold too much inside, you block new experiences, new emotions, new opportunities, and new clarity.
The mind cannot receive while it is overflowing.

But release clears space.

It creates room for:

- joy
- creativity
- love
- insight
- inspiration
- understanding
- courage
- self-compassion
- peace

This is why so much brilliance happens after relief.
People make life-changing decisions after emotional releases.
They find clarity after intense honesty.
They discover wisdom after crying.
They forgive themselves after acknowledging their truth.

Relief empties the cup.
Life fills it again.

Why Relief Feels Like Truth Arriving

Relief often brings sudden clarity:

"I finally know what I want."
"I finally understand what hurt me."
"I finally accept what happened."
"I finally feel like myself."

This clarity does not come from thinking.
It comes from **removing the blockages that were preventing you from seeing clearly**.

Imagine your mind as a window covered in dust.
When you wipe it clean (release),
the view returns.

Relief reveals truth.
Truth reveals direction.
Direction reveals peace.

There Is No Joy Quite Like the Joy of Letting Go

The joy of achieving something is powerful.
The joy of love is beautiful.
The joy of companionship is comforting.
The joy of success is motivating.

But there is a unique, incomparable joy that surpasses all others:

The joy of being unburdened.

It is the joy of:
"I am finally free from this weight.
I don't have to carry it anymore."

It is the joy of being lighter inside your own body.
Lighter inside your own thoughts.
Lighter inside your own life.

It is the joy of meeting yourself again.

Relief is the bridge between suffering and peace.
It is not the end of pain
it is the doorway out of it.

The Joy of Relief: A Summary in Feeling

Relief is:

- the breath after crying
- the calm after truth
- the softness after tension
- the clarity after confusion
- the acceptance after struggle
- the peace after resistance
- the quiet after storms
- the laughter after heaviness
- the exhale after holding yourself too tightly

Relief is the human reset button.
Not a luxury
a necessity.

Without release, no one can survive their own mind.
With release, anyone can transform their entire life.

"Relief is the universe reminding you that peace was always waiting just behind the weight you finally let go."

CHAPTER 15 The Flow Philosophy: Let What Comes Come, Let What Goes Go

The Ancient Art of Moving Through Life Without Drowning in It

There is a quiet wisdom running through the world, present in rivers, winds, seasons, and the way nature grows. It is the wisdom of **flow** the principle that life moves smoothly when nothing clings too tightly, resists too strongly, or holds too long. Human beings, however, are the only creatures who insist on grabbing what should pass, resisting what should unfold, and controlling what should naturally move.

A river does not argue with rocks.
A tree does not cling to old leaves.
The sun does not resist the setting.
Clouds do not negotiate their shapes.
Birds do not cling to broken branches.
Oceans do not hold every wave.

Only humans suffer because we hold life like a fist instead of letting it flow like open hands.

Flow is not passivity it is alignment.
It is the art of allowing life to move, internally and externally, without unnecessary force.
To live in flow is to stop fighting what is temporary and stop fearing what is new.

This chapter explores the philosophy that has guided mystics, monks, philosophers, and the happiest people across history:
Let what comes come. Let what goes go. Neither grasp nor resist. Let life breathe.

THE FIRST PRINCIPLE OF FLOW: Life Moves You Suffer When You Don't

Life is motion. It is never still.
Your thoughts move.
Your emotions move.
Your circumstances move.
Your identity evolves.
Your relationships shift.
Your desires grow and change.
Your seasons transform.
Your truths mature.

The only constant movement is change yet humans treat change as the enemy.

We suffer not because life moves,
but because we try to trap it in the shape we prefer.

Trying to freeze life is like trying to trap the wind in a bottle.
It will suffocate.
And so will you.

Flow requires allowing life to be what it is not what your fear, ego, or expectation demand it to be.

THE SECOND PRINCIPLE OF FLOW:
Release Is Natural Resistance Is Learned

Human beings are born in flow.
A baby cries, then laughs.
Feels fear, then forgets.
Feels hunger, then fullness.
Loves effortlessly.
Lets go instantly.
Is present endlessly.

It is adults who teach children how to hold emotions, suppress needs, overthink feelings, and resist change.

You learned resistance.
You learned emotional hoarding.
You learned mental clenching.
You learned fear of uncertainty.
You learned attachment to things that break your peace.

Flow is not something new you must acquire
it is your original nature, buried under layers of conditioned heaviness.

Letting go is not a skill you learn.
It is a memory you return to.

THE THIRD PRINCIPLE OF FLOW:
Thoughts and Emotions Are Guests, Not Furniture

A flowing mind treats thoughts like visitors.
They arrive.
They stay.
They leave.

A stuck mind treats thoughts like permanent tenants.
Fear becomes furniture.
Doubt becomes wallpaper.
Past mistakes become photo frames.

Flow is not about stopping thoughts, but about not trapping them.

Flow says:
"I see this thought. It may stay if it needs, but it will leave when it's done."

Flow requires trust:
that you can experience emotion without drowning in it,
that you can face truth without collapsing,
and that you can let go without losing anything meaningful.

In flow, everything knows how to move.
It is the mind that must remember.

THE FOURTH PRINCIPLE OF FLOW: Not Everything Deserves a Fight

Some things require effort.
Some things require patience.
Many things require no action at all.

But the ego loves to fight.
It wants to control every outcome, correct every person, win every argument, fix every problem, and predict every possibility.

Flow whispers:
"Not everything needs your interference."

Most conflicts in life dissolve on their own when you stop feeding them energy.
Most fears lose power when you stop rehearsing them.
Most problems shrink when you stop magnifying them through overthinking.

Flow requires the wisdom to know the difference between:

- what needs attention,
- what needs acceptance,
- and what needs to be left alone.

THE FIFTH PRINCIPLE OF FLOW: What Is Yours Will Stay Without Force

People often hold tightly out of fear fear of losing, fear of change, fear of uncertainty, fear of being alone. But whatever is truly meant for you will never require mental violence or emotional begging to remain.

Flow-based relationships are not based on gripping.
They are based on freedom.

If someone stays, it's because they choose to.
If someone leaves, it's because they are no longer aligned with your path.

Flow teaches you:
"Do not chase. Do not grip. Do not cling.
What is aligned will remain. What is not will release."

Gripping causes suffering.
Flow creates trust.

THE SIXTH PRINCIPLE OF FLOW: What Leaves Creates Space for What Arrives

Many people suffer because they confuse losing with emptiness. But emptiness is not the absence of value it is the presence of space. Space is potential. Space is possibility. Space is rebirth.

Every ending creates space for a beginning.
Every release creates space for renewal.

Every loss creates space for alignment.
Every closure creates space for clarity.

Flow asks you to trust the space.
Fear asks you to fill it immediately.

The universe operates like a river:
If water leaves, more water flows in.
If you make space, life fills it with something better aligned.

Flow is faith in motion.

THE SEVENTH PRINCIPLE OF FLOW: Peace Comes From Moving With Life, Not Against It

When you live in flow:

- you stop pushing
- you stop forcing
- you stop fighting reality
- you stop resisting the truth
- you stop clinging to the past
- you stop fearing the future
- you stop carrying expired emotions

Flow feels like breathing again.
Like exhaling after a long day.
Like relaxing into your own existence.
Like allowing life to unfold rather than micromanaging the universe.

Flow is the natural state of peace.
Resistance is the unnatural state of suffering.

Peace is not something you find
it is something you stop blocking.

THE PRACTICE OF FLOW: Let What Comes Come, Let What Goes Go

This is the simplest and hardest rule of life.

Let What Comes Come

Trust the arrival.
Trust the experience.
Trust the lesson.
Trust the timing.
Trust yourself to handle whatever enters your life.

Let What Goes Go

Release without bitterness.
Release without fear.
Release without chasing.
Release without questioning.
Trust that what leaves makes space.

Flow is not about being passive or detached
it is about being aligned.

When you let life flow, you stop drowning in what was
and start swimming in what is.

THE FREEDOM OF A FLOWING LIFE

A flowing life feels:

- lighter
- simpler
- softer
- wiser
- more peaceful
- more intuitive
- more spacious
- more joyful
- more aligned

You feel less fear and more trust.
You hold less and experience more.
You think less and understand more.
You resist less and receive more.

Flow doesn't guarantee perfection
it guarantees freedom.

Not freedom from life,
but freedom *within* life.

"Life becomes gentle the moment you stop gripping it. What comes comes. What goes goes. Peace lives in the space between."

CHAPTER 16   Think and Have Pee (The Final Realization)

The Wisdom of Release, the Humor of Being Human, and the Secret Behind a Free Mind

Every journey whether spiritual, philosophical, emotional, or hilariously human comes down to one fundamental truth:

Freedom begins the moment you stop holding what hurts and allow life to flow the way your body already understands.

The title of this book, "Think and Have Pee," was never about comedy alone. Yes, it's funny. Yes, it catches attention. Yes, it disarms seriousness. But beneath the humor lies a quiet brilliance:

Your body already knows what your mind struggles to learn.
When pressure builds, release is the only path to peace.

This final chapter brings everything together the science, the spirit, the psychology, the philosophy, the humor, and the humanity. It is not the end of the book. It is the beginning of your new way of thinking and living.

THE HUMAN BODY IS THE FIRST TEACHER OF LETTING GO

Long before you learned meditation, mantras, therapy, journaling, or spirituality...
your body taught you how to release pressure.

When your bladder fills, you feel discomfort.
When you hold it too long, the discomfort becomes pain.
When you finally release, the relief is immediate effortless, natural, cooling, calming.

This cycle is the blueprint for emotional and mental well-being:

- pressure builds
- discomfort rises
- avoidance hurts more
- release brings peace

The body does not complicate this process.
The mind is the one that interferes.

This book exists to teach your mind what your body already understands.

THE MIND MAKES EVERYTHING HEAVIER THAN NECESSARY

If your bladder worked the way your mind does, you would:

- question whether you *deserved* to go

- analyze who caused the pressure
- replay every past time you peed
- fear what will happen if you release
- compare your need to others
- hold it to avoid discomfort
- wait for a "perfect moment"
- tell yourself "I should be stronger"
- try distracting yourself
- pretend you don't feel pressure
- panic when pressure becomes unbearable

This is exactly how humans treat emotions.

We complicate what nature designed to be simple.

We hold anger.
We hold guilt.
We hold fear.
We hold memories.
We hold expectations.
We hold heartbreak.
We hold pressure that has long expired.

The body knows:
"You must release."
The mind says:
"Not yet. I'm scared."

And so suffering continues.

THE TRUE MEANING OF "THINK AND HAVE PEE"

At its core, the title is a formula:

1. THINK

Become aware of what you're holding.
Notice your pressure.
Understand your mental weight.
Acknowledge the emotions you bury.
Recognize the thoughts you grasp.
Awaken to your inner tension.

2. AND

Accept that life is a continuous flow.
Movement is normal.
Change is healthy.
Release is natural.

3. HAVE PEE

Let go emotionally, mentally, spiritually.
Release pressure the moment it hurts.
Flush what does not belong.
Empty the tank regularly.
Choose flow over force.
Choose peace over tension.

It sounds humorous, but it is the essence of mental health, spiritual growth, and emotional intelligence.

RELEASE IS WISDOM, NOT WEAKNESS

People often believe:

"I must be strong enough to hold everything."

No.
Strength is not in holding.
Strength is in knowing **when to release**.

A wise person doesn't grip life tightly.
A wise person lets life flow through them.

Release is not avoidance.
Release is not denial.
Release is not irresponsibility.

Release is the maturity to say:

- "This feeling has taught me enough."
- "This memory does not define me anymore."
- "This worry has no benefit."
- "This guilt has expired."
- "This fear does not belong to my future."

Letting go is emotional hygiene.
Without it, the mind becomes clogged.

THE SECRET TO A FREE MIND: REGULAR EMPTYING

Just as your body needs to release every day,
your mind needs it too.

Emotional release.
Mental release.
Spiritual release.

Not once a year.
Not during a breakdown.
Not only in crisis.

But daily.

Release is not an emergency action it is a lifestyle.

A free mind empties itself frequently so nothing becomes toxic.

Tension dissolves.
Pressure decreases.
Thoughts soften.
Life flows.

HUMOR MAKES THE JOURNEY LIGHTER

The reason humor is woven into this philosophy is simple:

People learn better when they're not terrified of their own feelings.

A heavy message becomes lighter with humor.
A painful truth becomes digestible with playfulness.
A serious insight becomes relatable with a smile.

Humor breaks the ego.
Humor melts resistance.

Humor opens the heart.
Humor allows wisdom to enter without force.

If enlightenment is a mountain,
humor is the elevator.

YOU ARE NOT SUPPOSED TO SUFFER THROUGH PRESSURE

This book wasn't written to entertain.
It was written to transform.

To help you understand:

- your emotions are natural
- your pressure is not a flaw
- your discomfort is a signal
- your mind doesn't need to hold everything
- your heart is allowed to release
- your soul grows when it lets go

You deserve peace not because you earned it,
but because you are a human being with a mind that moves.

You deserve release not because life is perfect,
but because life is always changing.

You deserve relief not because pressure is wrong,
but because pressure is temporary.

THE FINAL REALIZATION

Here is the truth this entire book has been leading you toward:

Peace is not something you find it is something you create by emptying what blocks it.

You don't need to become enlightened.
You don't need to meditate for years.
You don't need to read every philosophy.
You don't need to perfect your mind.

You only need to do what your body already knows:

Feel the pressure.
Acknowledge it.
Release it.
Return to flow.

This is the wisdom of "Think and Have Pee."
It is a philosophy disguised as humor.
A spiritual truth wrapped in laughter.
A psychological guide wearing a funny title.
A simple invitation:

Stop holding what hurts.
Start flowing with what heals.

Life becomes peaceful when you stop carrying expired weight.
Life becomes joyful when you allow yourself to release.
Life becomes meaningful when you let wisdom flow through you.

You were never meant to hold everything inside.
You were meant to think...
and then let go.

"A free mind is not the one that thinks the most it's the one that releases the fastest."

EPILOGUE

When the Mind Finally Breathes

In the end, life is not a race or a puzzle or a test of endurance.
Life is a rhythm a pulse that grows quieter when you stop fighting it.
A flow that becomes clearer when you stop holding everything inside.

You were never meant to carry your thoughts like a burden,
your emotions like a locked vault,
your past like a chained anchor.

This book was a reminder that peace is not earned
peace is restored by release.

You do not heal by gripping.
You heal by loosening.
You rise by softening.
You grow by flowing.
You become yourself again by finally letting go
of everything that was never yours to hold.

If there is one promise I hope lives inside you long after the pages fade, it is this:

Your mind is allowed to be light.
Your heart is allowed to be free.
And you beautifully, imperfectly human
are allowed to release whenever life becomes too heavy.

In that release, you will rediscover the person you were always meant to be
someone unburdened, someone spacious, someone alive.

Think clearly.
Feel deeply.
Release often.
Flow always.

The rest will take care of itself.

AUTHOR'S NOTE

I did not write this book to preach.
I wrote it because I have lived the weight of a mind that holds too much,
and I have lived the freedom of a mind that finally lets go.

I wrote it because humans are funny.
We complicate what nature already made simple.
We laugh at the idea of release,
yet we suffer because we refuse to practice it.

I wrote it because humor softens the heart,
and softened hearts are the doorway to wisdom.

If this book made you laugh, reflect, release, breathe,
or see your mind with kinder eyes
then it has done the work it was born to do.

Carry nothing that suffocates your peace.
Hold nothing that blocks your clarity.
And when life begins to weigh down your spirit, remember:
You already know what to do.
Think... and have pee.
Release the pressure.
Return to yourself.

Thank you for reading.
Thank you for trusting me to speak to your inner world.
And thank you truly for being human with me.

Shamail Aijaz

DEDICATION PAGE

To every human being who has ever held too much inside
may this book teach you to release sooner,
lighten your heart,
and laugh your way back to peace.

And to the beautiful mind reading this:

You deserve a life that feels light.
May you always remember how to let go.

FURTHER READING BY SHAMAIL AIJAZ

Explore More Books by the Author

If you enjoyed *Think and Have Pee* and wish to continue your journey into clarity, leadership, personal growth, emotional mastery, and mental freedom, the following books by **Shamail Aijaz** offer deeper insights, frameworks, and life-changing perspectives.

BUSINESS, LEADERSHIP & DECISION-MAKING

- **The Manager's Compass: Mastering Decisions, Time, and Impact**

A practical guide to leadership clarity, strategic thinking, and effective execution.

- **Paralyzed by Planning: How Businesses Waste Millions Before They Even Begin**

A deep dive into planning traps, analysis paralysis, and recovering momentum.

- **The Art of Risk: How Smart Businesses Prevent Chaos Before It Happens**

A masterclass in risk management, anticipation, and strategic prevention.

- **Standard Operating Excellence: The Complete Guide to Building, Implementing, and Mastering SOPs**

The ultimate manual for systems, processes, and organizational discipline.

• The Shape of Talent Framework: Redefining Skills, Growth, and Collaboration in the Modern Workforce

A new model for developing multidimensional talent in fast-changing environments.

MINDSET, PERSONAL GROWTH & HUMAN BEHAVIOR

• The Calm Within the Storm: Leading Beyond Ego

A book about emotional clarity, inner leadership, and navigating pressure with wisdom.

• Be You!: What They Hate in You Is Missing in Them

A transformational guide to authenticity, confidence, and personal alignment.

• The Myth of the Safe Path: How Playing Small Costs More Than Risk

A book that challenges comfort zones, fear narratives, and the illusion of safety.

• Dopamine: The Silent Architect of Desire, Discipline, and Meaning

A scientific and philosophical exploration of dopamine and human motivation.

DIGITAL STRATEGY, MARKETING & FUTURE OF WORK

- **Mastering Digital Campaigns: How Strategy, Data, and Design Drive Conversions**

A complete roadmap to high-performance digital marketing.

- **The Future of Learning with AI: Teaching the Mind, Saving the Human**

A look into how AI will reshape learning, thinking, and human potential.

- **Neuromarketing Made Simple** *(If included in your catalog)*

Explaining the psychology behind consumer decisions and persuasive communication.

Printed in Dunstable, United Kingdom